Other titles in the A Retreat With... *Series:*

Mother Teresa and Damien of Molokai: Caring for Those Who Suffer,
  by Joan Guntzelman

Oscar Romero and Dorothy Day: Walking With the Poor,
  by Marie Dennis

Our Lady of Guadalupe and Juan Diego: Heeding the Call,
  by Virgilio Elizondo and Friends

Our Lady, Dominic and Ignatius: Praying With Our Bodies, by
  Betsey Beckman, Nina O'Connor and J. Michael Sparough, S.J.

Patrick: Discovering God in All, by Timothy Joyce, O.S.B.

Pope John XXIII: Opening the Windows to Wisdom, by Alfred McBride,
  O. Praem.

Teresa of Avila: Living by Holy Wit, by Gloria Hutchinson

Thea Bowman and Bede Abram: Leaning On the Lord,
  by Joseph A. Brown, S.J.

Therese of Lisieux: Loving Our Way Into Holiness,
  by Elizabeth Ruth Obbard, O.D.C.

Thomas Merton: Becoming Who We Are, by Dr. Anthony T. Padovano

A RETREAT WITH
EDITH STEIN

Trusting God's Purpose

Patricia L. Marks

ST. ANTHONY MESSENGER PRESS

Cincinnati, Ohio

*Dedicated to
all catechists and
healers who have
sustained me.
Especially M. and L.*

Scripture citations are taken from the *New Revised Standard Version Bible*, copyright ©1989 by the Division of Christian Education of the National Council of Churches of Christ in the U.S.A. and used by permission.

Excerpts from *The Hidden Life*, translated by Waltraut Stein, Ph. D. ©1992; *Essays On Woman, Volume Two of the Collected Works of Edith Stein*, ©1987; *Life in a Jewish Family*, translated by Josephine Koeppel, O.C.D. ©1986; *On the Problem of Empathy*, translated by Waltraut Stein, Ph. D. ©1989; and *Self-Portrait in Letters: 1916-1942*, translated by Josephine Koeppel, O.C.D., ©1983, are used by permission of the Washington Province of Discalced Carmelites, ICS Publications 2131 Lincoln Rd. N.E. Washington, D.C. 20002-1199, U.S.A.

Excerpts from *Edith Stein, Selected Writings: With Comments Reminiscences and Translations of Her Poems and Prayers by Her Niece*, by Susanne M. Batzdorff, ©1990, are used by permission of Templegate Publishers.

Excerpts from *Prayer, Humility and Compassion*, by Samuel H. Dresner, ©1957, are used by permission of the Jewish Publication Society of America.

Cover illustration by Steve Erspamer, S.M.
Cover and book design by Mary Alfieri

ISBN 0-86716-387-9

Copyright ©2001, Patricia L. Marks

Published by St. Anthony Messenger Press
www.AmericanCatholic.org
Printed in the U.S.A.

Contents

Introducing A Retreat With...

Several years ago, Gloria Hutchinson took up the exhortation once given to Thomas Merton: "Keep on writing books that make people love the spiritual life." Through her own writing and that of many gifted others, Gloria brought flesh and format to this retreat series.

It is with a deep appreciation for her foresight that I have assumed the role of series editor. Those of you who have returned to this series again and again will not be jarred by the changes; they are few and subtle. Those of you who are new will find, I hope, that God works to reach us in any manner we will permit, if we but take the time to come aside for a while and wait for the spirit.

The many mentors who have come to life in the pages of this series are not meant to be a conglomeration of quotes by and about them. They are intimate portraits, drawn by authors who know their subject well. But just as our viewing of the Mona Lisa tells us more about ourselves than about Leonardo's relationship with his mysterious subject, so the real value in these retreats comes from the minds and hearts of their readers. You are invited to dream and doubt, muse and murmur. If you find a mentor's words compelling, the end of each book has a list of resources to deepen your acquaintance. If you find some of your mentor's ideas challenging, or even disturbing, you can be sure the spirit is at work.

Come aside for a while...

Kathleen Carroll
Series Editor

1

Getting to Know Our Director

Introducing Edith

Edith Stein was the youngest of eleven children born to Siegfried and Auguste Stein. Seven survived—two boys and five girls. Erna and Edith, the two youngest, became inseparable. Edith had a passionate interest in learning and sustained her commitment to it. She was also blessed with an extraordinary memory. These gifts remained with her to the last.

The Stein family suffered the same contradictions and weaknesses found in all families. Edith's niece, Susanne Batzdorff (daughter of Edith's sister Erna and Hans Biberstein), recounts, for example:

> The small annoyances stemming from these differences in their temperament and makeup [Auguste and those who married her children] apparently fueled a constant climate of irritability and conflict which were detrimental to domestic tranquillity *(shalom bayit)*, a very important concept in Judaism.[1]

In family life, we find deep joy and strong frustrations. There are both admirable traits and grating characteristics to be found in those we love and live with closely.

Edith was always a fierce servant of truth and would be the first to protest a falsely positive portrayal of her life. Despite Edith's closeness to her mother, there were aspects of her daughter about which Auguste never learned. Edith writes candidly and clearly—but rarely—about her inner sufferings. Only since the turn of the twentieth century have scholars begun to find the inner lives of children significant. Interestingly, strongly spiritual people often comment about early hints of future deep understandings of God, faith and interiority. Thus, the following account of Edith's inner struggle at so young an age is refreshing, instructive and helpful. She writes about herself around the ages of six and seven:

> Despite this intimate bond [between herself and her mother], my mother was not my confidante. I went through sudden transition, incomprehensible to the observer.... I would lie on the floor stiff with resistance...screaming at the top of my lungs.... Within me there was a hidden world.... The sight of a drunkard could...plague me for nights on end... for no apparent reason I sometimes developed a fever and in delirium spoke of the things that were oppressing me inwardly. The first great transformation took place in me when I was about seven years old.... I cannot explain it otherwise than that reason assumed command within me...from that time on, I was convinced that my mother and my sister Frieda had a better knowledge of what was good for me than I had.... Gradually my inner world grew lighter and clearer.[2]

She had become phobic and panicky about any accounts of violence and murder. The knowledge that human beings are capable of despicable actions toward one another was a sad and difficult revelation for her. Until the time she first wrote of these things in 1933, it seems she kept all this suffering to herself. How little did she then realize the utter importance of learning to yield to trust and calm. How telling and poignant that while still so young she wrestled with a fear of violence being done to herself and to others.

Very early on, Edith developed passions for friendship and scholarship. She saw every relationship as serious and remained fiercely loyal to her friends. When relationships were broken off, it was rare that Edith had ended them. In 1925, at age thirty-four, she writes to Fritz Kaufmann:

> The formation of an unshakable bond with all whom life brings in my way, a bond in no way dependent on day-to-day contact, is a significant element in my life. And you can depend on that tie even when I do not always reply as promptly as this time.[3]

Edith was headstrong in all her endeavors. In her youth, the negative side of her enduring loyalty was a stubbornness in favor of her own perspective. At age fifteen, Edith announced to her mother that she was leaving school and giving up prayer. Some refer to this as her atheistic period. But many believe this characterization to be too strong for someone who may simply have turned away out of boredom, distraction or ignorance. Off she went to her sister Else in Hamburg to help her raise the children and keep house. Less than a year later, however, she decided to return home and continue her schooling.

Her distance from prayer and belief, though, continued for some years. Philosophy became her locus of truth, and she threw herself into her studies resolutely. Edith managed to achieve a prominent spot among the male majority of philosophy students at the University of Breslau, and later at Göttingen and Freiburg. She does not divulge many details of close relationships she may have had during that time but hints at normal desires and wishes. In *Life in a Jewish Family*, she says, "It happened, at times, that I found among my associates a young man whom I liked very much and whom I could imagine as a future life-partner. But hardly anyone was aware of this."[4]

There are a few references to Hans Lipp, for whom she dearly cared. Lipp later married and was killed in World War I. Edith also was close to Hans Biberstein, who later became her brother-in-law. They retained a close, lifelong friendship despite the war, the Bibersteins' move to America and Edith's entry into Carmel.

On August 3, 1916, when Edith was twenty-four, the great phenomenologist Edmund Husserl informed her that her Ph.D. in philosophy had been awarded *summa cum laude* from the University of Freiburg in Breisgau. Her dissertation was a phenomenological explanation of the nature of empathy. After receiving her doctorate, Edith hoped to obtain a habilitation—a teaching post at a major university. As the years went on, she realized that being a Jew and a woman in a Germany with a worsening political and social climate would prohibit her the advancement she desired and deserved. These situations caused her suffering, yet she persisted in whatever way possible to obtain her dreams. She even hoped that the two years she spent helping Husserl arrange his papers and writings would smooth the way for her acceptance somewhere within the German university system. It did not.

To some, Edith appeared austere and aloof, deeply involved in her studies and thoughts. Those, however, who gained her friendship mention an affectionate nature and loyalty as two hallmarks of her personality. She had a love for nature, for scholarship, for both serious and lively conversation, and as her philosophical writings show, she had a deeply reflective mind. Edith's relatives and biographers write of her sense of humor, her penchant for humorous plays and skits, and a love of laughter. Her friends and relatives feared that a life in Carmel would cloud her sharp mind and loving disposition with gloom and heaviness. This was not at all the case. Sister Josephine Koeppel recounts several instances of Sister Benedicta's hearty laughter, with others and at herself.

> Sister Benedicta was anything but a sanctimonious, nearly perfect, stereotypical novice. Her wit was as lively at the age of forty-two as it had been in her

teens: her gift for mimicry enabled her to copy the
behavior and attitudes of her companions in the
novitiate so well that those she was teasing felt
complimented and joined in the hearty laughter.[5]

Toward Christianity

Susanne Batzdorff feels that Edith knew very little
about her Jewish religious heritage. She grew up in a
brief period of relative freedom for Jews in Germany.
Perhaps, then, she embraced ideas and possibilities of
social progress. Though she attended synagogue with
her mother, she was never schooled in her faith. When
Edith got to the University of Göttingen her friends
were mostly Christians and converted Jews. Susanne
wonders if Edith might not have converted, had she had
more exposure to the Jewish faith. We cannot know these
things, of course, but it is important to understand these
aspects of Edith's life and how her own family members
view her. Susanne's book *Aunt Edith: The Jewish Heritage
of a Catholic Saint* shows us the struggle she and her
family have gone through over the life, conversion, death
and use of Edith Stein by the world and the Church.

Edith Stein's journey through her studies, her
giftedness in human relationships and the circumstances
of her life led her to Christ and to the Church. One of her
most respected professors was Adolf Reinach, a Lutheran
Christian who was killed in 1917. When Edith journeyed
to comfort the widow of this dearly loved teacher, she
found a woman deeply convinced of the power of Christ's
victory over death and suffering. Edith had admired
Reinach's personal goodness as much as his scholarship
and was profoundly influenced by Frau Reinach's faith in
Jesus. This visit was to be extremely important in Edith's
own faith journey. This experience led her to what would

become such an important facet of her own spirituality—
the suffering of Jesus. She wrote:

> Bound to him, you are omnipresent as he is. You
> cannot help here or there like the physician, the
> nurse, the priest. You can be at all fronts, wherever
> there is grief, in the power of the cross. Your
> compassionate love takes you everywhere, this love
> from the divine heart.[6]

These are the words of a person whose sense of empathy
was deep and strong. Edith's acceptance and embrace of
Jesus' encounter with human suffering led her to a deeper
understanding of the purpose of life on earth.

Teresa of Avila also profoundly influenced Edith.
In the summer of 1921, Edith read Teresa's *The Book of
Her Life*. This reading was an epiphany for Edith and
cemented her decision to enter the Catholic Church,
which she did on January 1, 1922. Edith also tells us
that she perceived a vocation to Carmel the very day of
her Baptism. But Edith's conversion was a great trauma
for her mother. It was a significant challenge for both
of them to maintain their loving relationship and an
immediate entrance into Carmel could only cause further
strain. Also, Edith was a new convert and Church law
forbade her entry into a religious congregation for at least
three years. Her spiritual director cautioned her to wait,
realizing the contribution she had to make as a teacher,
lecturer and writer. She delayed her entry for nine years.

Edith's conversion made her an apostate to the Jewish
faith and caused confusion and deep pain for her and
her family. It is often difficult for us to understand and
respect another's transcendent call. How necessary, then,
that we develop a certain comfort with ambiguity and
differences of a sacred nature. In the end, none of us can
know God's mind and intent.

Edith's World

In July 1998, Pope John Paul II chose Respect for Human Rights: The Secret of True Peace as the theme for the thirty-second World Day of Peace celebrated January 1, 1999. The Holy Father reflected:

> Peace is not imposed; it rises instead from the heart of every individual, every human community, and aims at the good of all. Respect for the rights of individuals and of every people therefore guarantees and promotes true peace.[7]

The respect for human rights of which the Pope speaks will sometimes bring over us a puzzled and painful silence: We cannot know the whys and wherefores of God's action in the lives of our brothers and sisters. What we need to respect in each other, though it is not without its difficulties, is the transcendent call each person follows. By structure and polity we do not control God's spirit or actions. Any religious conviction that winds up condemning whole classes of people must be firmly and decidedly rejected. Unlike many others who followed religious calls that took them far from their beginnings, Edith Stein offers us no detailed account of her inner motivation, intent and reasons in moving from Judaism to Christianity. We may conjecture that in her attraction to Teresa of Avila, who loved God completely, she found a kindred soul whose devotion was genuine and deep. We must find her greatness in her actions and interactions with others. This intelligent woman lived amid political instability and anti-Semitism. This latent prejudice eventually became overt and terrifying. She had to move about with increasingly less security. She did not have the luxury of developing her thought and spirituality into old age. Like that of millions, her life and time were stolen. How impoverished are we all, deprived of their gifts!

If faith for Jews is different after Auschwitz, so is it also for Christians who live after the Holocaust. It is we who must admit that attitudes that began long ago in our history and theology developed into a tragic but historically traceable path of anti-Judaism that made the Holocaust possible. It is to be hoped we have learned never again to trust any triumphalism that sees any class of persons as fair game for exclusion, genocide or displacement. Each human person, created in God's image, is a prism through which we somehow encounter the divine. Held up to the light of the Holy One's enduring love, we, each a precious work of God, spread colored streams, varied and beautiful, into the heart of the beholder. Peace resides in that place beyond even our worthy and sacred differences where we all exist in the unchanging regard of our creator.

Notes

[1] Susanne Batzdorff, *Aunt Edith: The Jewish Heritage of a Catholic Saint* (Springfield, Ill.: Templegate Publishers, 1998), pp. 7–8.

[2] Edith Stein, *Life in a Jewish Family: 1891–1916*, vol. 1, *Collected Works of Edith Stein*, trans. Josephine Koeppel, O.C.D. (Washington, D.C.: ICS Publications, 1986), pp. 73–75.

[3] Edith Stein, *Self-Portrait in Letters: 1916–1942*, vol. 5, *Collected Works of Edith Stein*, trans. Josephine Koeppel, O.C.D. (Washington, D.C.: ICS Publications, 1993), p. 46.

[4] Stein, *Life in a Jewish Family*, p. 227.

[5] Josephine Koeppel, O.C.D., *Edith Stein: Philosopher and Mystic* (Collegeville, Minn.: The Liturgical Press, 1990), p. 139.

[6] Edith Stein, *The Hidden Life: Essays, Meditations, Spiritual Texts*, vol. 4, *Collected Works of Edith Stein*, trans. Waltraut Stein, Ph.D. (Washington, D.C.: ICS Publications, 1992), p. 96.

[7] *L'Osservatore Romano*.

DAY ONE

Setting Our Faces
Toward Jerusalem

Introducing Our Retreat Theme

God is all around us, whispering, shouting, luring
in the passion of creation. God beckons in the faces of
children and seeks our love in the very real needs of
human persons. God has blessed our nature and our
needs, identifying with the least and thus with all. In
the Torah we hear it as the foundation of human history:
"Hear, O Israel: The LORD is our God, the LORD alone.
You shall love the LORD your God with all your heart, and
with all your soul, and with all your might" (Deuteronomy
6:4–5). And, "You shall love your neighbor as yourself: I
am the LORD" (Leviticus 19:18). God's sovereignty frames
the discussion and the task. The Holy One has asked for
love, commanded love, made love the standard against
which we enter into the safety of divine union. The more
we grasp this presence of God and live in it, the more we
are living at God's hand, trusting God's purpose.

How do we live at God's hand? It is our obedience
that allows God's embrace, as it were. In our trust we find
our fidelity. Faithful action toward the good of all is the
return we make to the creator of all. To live at God's hand
means we paint our life stories with whatever pigments
our circumstances allow. We find joy where many think

joy cannot be found. We find meaning and grace that make the totality of our lives, however humble, stronger than death itself. In love and trust, we learn that suffering can lead ultimately to glory and fulfillment.

Sitting in loving attentiveness to the Spirit is pausing and reflecting at God's hand. We can become aware of that power surrounding and permeating us like soft dew on spring grass. In becoming one with the neighbors whose lives and needs pass before us each day, we are living at God's hand. When we give and receive in a cycle of care that includes God, ourselves and others, this is the locus of God's will. Should God demand great things, God will supply great means. Should God ask us only to pick up a pin, hold a door or smile at another, we are living at God's hand. All the good that we do lives for eternity in the mystery of God's truth.

Opening Prayer

Who are you, sweet light, that fills me
And illumines the darkness of my heart?
You lead me like a mother's hand,
And should you let go of me,
I would not know how to take another step.
You are the space
That embraces my being and buries it in yourself.
Away from you it sinks into the abyss
Of nothingness, from which you raised it to
   the light.
You, nearer to me than I to myself
And more interior than my most interior
And still impalpable and intangible
And beyond any name:
Holy Spirit, eternal love![1]

RETREAT SESSION ONE
Understanding God's Will

Everyone who journeys toward God struggles to understand God's will. Finding the purpose of our own journey weighs daily upon our hearts and minds. The prophets themselves questioned their callings. Jeremiah called himself a man of unclean lips. Isaiah felt he was too young for God's task. Jesus himself recoiled at the thought of the suffering that lay before him. Our forebears from the earliest times have given us an example of searching and seeking that encourages. It is important to recall that God's purposes are not limited by our weaknesses and sins. At the very beginning, we must fully accept our own limitations and those of others as part of discerning, knowing and doing God's will.

We know that God is ever present and acting, helping us see and understand. We can trust in this. In the process of our retreat some bit of God's leading will become known to each of us. The journey is easier when it can be shared, but it is still possible when those closest to us fail.

In embarking upon this retreat, we have set our faces toward Jerusalem. We pass through our earthly cities, our time-restricted lives, to the joys of life everlasting—the heavenly Jerusalem. Spend some time with the wealth of this image: Jerusalem—David's city, the seat of Judah, home of the ark and then of the temple. Her inhabitants both accepted and stoned the prophets. Jerusalem was always a city of both woe and exultation. Her earth absorbed the blood of so many unjustly slain. Jerusalem—a multifaceted reality, so much like the complex reality of human life, growth and experience.

Jesus' whole life was doing God's will; accomplishing that for which he was sent. In the fourth chapter of John we can see how others, unsuspecting at first, came to realize that the truths of Jesus break into their lives suddenly, and lovingly and point them in a totally new direction.

> A Samaritan woman came to draw water, and Jesus said to her, "Give me a drink." (His disciples had gone to the city to buy food.) The Samaritan woman said to him, "How is it that you, a Jew, ask a drink of me, a woman of Samaria?" (Jews do not share things in common with Samaritans.) Jesus answered her, "If you knew the gift of God, and who it is that is saying to you, 'Give me a drink,' you would have asked him, and he would have given you living water." (John 4:7–9)

So many things to say about this passage! It is both consoling and challenging. Jesus is tired from his travels. Fatigue was one of the numerous human things that Jesus embraced in becoming flesh like us. Still "his food"was to know and do the will of the One who sent him. His passion is to complete the work that the Father has asked of him. Despite his weariness, Jesus does not let an opportunity pass to open eyes and influence hearts concerning the life that his teaching brings. The traditional antinomy between Samaritans and Jews does not deter him. Nor does he adhere to the convention that forbids his speaking to a woman in public. God's will takes precedence over custom. When the woman took her usual trip to the well that day, little did she know that her whole life would be changed through this encounter. She would become a disciple by day's end!

Reflect for a moment how God uses common things, usual encounters, routine people, tasks and human relationships to accomplish God's will. We can expect God to speak to our hearts at any time, in any place. God our Creator does not disdain mortal means. Jesus who endured the horror of crucifixion teaches that even in ignominy God's purposes may be served. God's purpose sometimes demands a trust that must run counter to all that is tangible or apparent. Jesus asks the Samaritan woman for a drink. Her reply indicates surprise that he, a male and a Jew would address her at all and in public, much less ask something from her. What Jesus promises is momentarily beyond her comprehension.

We are often like the Samaritan woman. Jesus speaks to us but we do not initially comprehend the depth and the promise. We have become so used to our preconceived notions of God and others that we may be unable to hear. We are, perhaps, too sure of what God wants from us and how God ought to accomplish good through us. What we learn from this encounter of Jesus and the woman at the well is to understand God's will for us by entering deeply into the reality of our own lives in complete trust.

Each human life is bounded by a set of limitations that characterize life in this world. We are born with a particular genetic makeup. We live in a particular place during political and social circumstances that we did not create and may not want. But this limitation does not thwart God who entered our story and "pitched a tent among us." We initially understand our own journey by accepting what is. Jesus promises living water. He then tells the woman: "Everyone who drinks of this water will be thirsty again, but those who drink of the water that I will give them will never be thirsty. The water that I will give will become in them a spring of water gushing to eternal life" (John 4:13-14).

When Jesus speaks about living water, the woman at the well is interested, but still does not comprehend the awesome gift of which he speaks. She feels, perhaps, that this living water will make her life easier, and save her from the inconvenience of having to come again and again to the well. But she can only think in terms of her own limitations and modest ways of overcoming them. This is often true of us, too.

For example, after I graduated with my Ph.D. I assumed I would have a professorship at a major university. At that time God's will did not even enter into my plans or desires. Only when I finally, fully understood God's love did God's will interest me.

We know God's will in a general sense from the Scriptures. God acts through history. We have seen this with the Israelites, and in the life, example and teaching of Jesus. Love of God and neighbor are central. We know the importance of prayer and of works of mercy and loving kindness.

It is often easier to see God's will by seeing what it is *not*. All around us, people struggle with the sad consequences of selfishness. Because we are all created in God's image we realize that prejudice, slander, injustice, genocide and greed are not God's will. In any circumstances, we know that God desires goodness, even heroism, from us. Wrong does not become right based on the fickle whims of shifting fortunes and fads.

As to what each of us must do specifically within our own selves and circumstances—this becomes a matter for thought, prayer, consultation, self-knowledge and decision-making. We have been given intelligence and freedom, and the exercise of these give glory to God. There are many examples from the gospels that show Jesus' utter respect for our human freedom. In the case of the rich young man, Jesus offers a special invitation to become an apostle (Mark 10:13-16, Luke 18:15-17, Matthew 19:16-26). The young man cannot leave his possessions and chooses not to accept the Lord's gracious invitation. Jesus respects the man's freedom. Another example takes place in Luke 24 with the disciples on the road to Emmaus. At one point Jesus acts as if he will go on alone and they invite him to stay with them. (cf. Luke 24:28-29) What if they had not invited him?

We seldom reflect on the power *we* have, the power God has created in us. Many of the saints comment on how our *wanting* God draws God to us. There is never relationship without desire. God woos us into intimacy. Perhaps a thought will come into our minds and not leave it. Life may become empty and dissatisfying. There will be something missing, and it may take time and experience to realize that only God fills this space. Should grace be given us to live out God's love in the uniqueness of our circumstances, personalities and talents, then we need to spend time in prayer, reflection and spiritual reading and meditation. Consult with wise, level-headed, prayerful people. God may bring unexpected spiritual guides onto your path. You will find those who will lead you and those you are called upon to lead. Whisper always in your heart: "God, lead me in pleasing you. Let me know what I ought to do for your glory, the love of others and the eternal salvation of my soul." A call becomes an integral part of one's personality, like the melodic theme of a symphony.

Remember, though, that not all teachings are subject to change or personal interpretation. Are we ever free of forgiving one another? Can we be released from the works of mercy? Do we qualify at any time to take God's right of judgment away? Paul says, "One sows, another reaps, but God gives the increase." With the shortness of life we come to realize that many significant changes do not happen within one life span. We are reaping what others have sown, and we are sowing what others will harvest.

When we pray that God's will be known and loved, and that all people will somehow come to know God's love, and that we may be the instruments for this, we are going in the right way. No foolishness or error of ours, sad as these may be, can separate us ultimately from God's love. Even horrors of history that we can hardly countenance cannot still the hand of God's mighty purposes.

Let us return now to Jesus at the well. After he makes the comment about living water (John 6:14) Jesus says that the hour is coming when we will worship not on Mount Geritzim or in Jerusalem but in "spirit and truth" (John 6:24). The gospel writer, then, connects true worship to the acceptance of Jesus. To worship in spirit and in truth is to render praise with the very person of Jesus. The Samaritan woman and her friends realize that the promised salvation is near in this person—Jesus—who offers new life, living water, fountains of grace, streams of God's presence to any and all who desire it. The woman has somehow grasped the enormity of all this and excitedly brings others to hear as well.

We might well ask "How did God's will become known to the Samaritan woman, and what seems to have been God's unique purpose for her?" She encounters God in the usual, perhaps boring, routine of going to the well to draw water. She responds with brashness to a stranger's simple request. But Jesus is not intimidated by her attitude or her situation. He is determined to reveal to her the wonder that has broken into the world through him. It is in Jesus' honest comments about her sin that she finds some handle of respect on which to grab hold as she senses excitement rising in her very being. Mantra-like she must have repeated, "He told me everything I have ever done!" (John 4:39) Through Jesus' love, conviction of sin brings relief from pain. Burdens are lifted, not imposed. The gift of cleansing enthuses the soul. God's purpose, "the gathering of fruit for eternal life" (John 4:36) is being accomplished through the woman's yes to truth, her admission of her own sin, and willingness to share the good message. Jesus, whose "food is to do the will of the One who sent Him," exults that an object of his love responds with joy. The manifestation of God's will, namely, *that we bear fruit,* is demonstrated in and through the woman herself. No aspect of her person is excluded in the doing of God's will.

It is so with us as individuals and as members of a faith community. We are fond of picking situations and lifestyles that are more reflective of God and goodness. This can be a dangerous enterprise. My particular journey took me through life in a Jewish family, the university, Carmel and a hateful political-historical situation. It was mine to seek God and respond in my circumstances to the primacy of love for God. My state of life is not what rejoices or displeases God. It is the witness to God's love and care that determines whether or not I imitated Jesus.

Be expectant about God's revelation of the unique truth of your life. Within the safety of the Scriptures and the wisdom of the faith community, bear fruit for God. Use God's gifts to begin anew each day, seeking the will of God as if nothing had yet been started. That is God's will! Let living water flow from you. Commit anew each day to the realities with which God surrounds you. May your very presence be an experience of love for others!

Jesus has set his face toward Jerusalem and he will not be deterred. He will not be hindered by our sin, our circumstances or our limitations. With new eyes we can see and trust God's power. We can rest in God, who is not bound by our human definitions of accomplishment and success. We can draw upon God's strength, undeterred even by frightening limitations within and about. No evil eclipses God's work or dampens God's passion to wrest good from the wreckage of human frailty.

For Reflection

- *What is clearer now for you concerning God's will? What action can you now take regarding God's will that you were unable to follow up to this point?*

- *The Samaritan woman was changed unexpectedly by her encounter with Jesus. "He told me everything I ever did!" she said. What has Jesus said to you about everything you have ever done?*

- *As you set your face toward Jerusalem, what clarity, strength and direction do you need the most? Ask this with confidence from the Lord who promises living water.*

Closing Prayer

We recall God's faithfulness long ago, and hope in this same help for ourselves. Holy Spirit, lead us this day and every day to see your presence both in hope's promise and its fulfillment, in what is and in what has not yet come to be.

Notes

1 Edith Stein, *From a Pentecost Novena, The Collected Works of Edith Stein* (Washington, D.C.: ICS Publications, 1989).

DAY TWO

The Person and Right Relationship

"You shall love your neighbor as yourself."
—Leviticus 19:18, Mark 12:30

Coming Together in the Spirit

In *Jewish Renewal*, Michael Lerner offers an explanation for the roots of violence. He retells the biblical account of Cain and Abel, making particular note of Cain's question to God, "Am I my brother's keeper?" He continues:

> Torah's unmistakable implication is that the moment one recognizes one's "other," one must simultaneously recognize the obligation toward caring and mutual concern.... Cruelty is made possible when human beings do not recognize in one another the image of God that is the essence of their own being—and hence turn away from others; do not hear their pain. Once this process begins, it builds upon itself, becomes a powerful force that is transferred from generation to generation. The people living in material abundance, fearful that they will not have enough if they share with everyone who is hungry, protect themselves from knowing others' pain by allowing themselves to believe that these are not human beings like themselves.[1]

Opening Prayer

Are you not the sweet manna
That from the Son's heart
Overflows into my heart,
The food of angels and the blessed?
He who raised himself from death to life,
He has also awakened me to new life
From the sleep of death.

And he gives me new life from day to day,
And at some time his fullness is to stream
    through me,
Life of your life indeed, you yourself:
Holy Spirit eternal life![2]

RETREAT SESSION TWO
I and Thou Revisited

All world conflicts begin somehow in the individual
heart and soul. Fed on ignorance, some absorb and
perpetuate demeaning stereotypes of others. We have
all seen instances in which these stereotypes are used to
justify inequitable treatment, cruel humor or fearful acts
of self-preservation. Far too many times and places have
seen these ideas used to justify acts of violence, murder
and genocide. But we must not despair when we are
surrounded by such evil. We must turn to God and trust
that good will come of it in the end. *"The greatest figures
of prophecy and sanctity step forth out of the darkest night...
Certainly the decisive turning points in world history are
substantially co-determined by souls whom no history book ever
mentions. And we will only find out about those souls to whom*

we owe the decisive turning points in our personal lives on the day when all that is hidden is revealed."[3]

It is a real puzzlement that twentieth-century science and psychology have made such great strides in understanding the human person, yet more people have been murdered in modern times than in any other historical epoch. In these times we have seen the Holocaust, prejudice and ethnic murders on a grand scale. Love has been all but lost in political and ideological upheavals. Hatred has become a fetid cul de sac of the soul. We find that our bad habits are institutionalized, historicized and passed down from generation to generation. Such a perversion of God's intent is what ultimately causes genocide, ethnic cleansing and holocausts.

We are easily distracted by the persistence of human imperfection and sinfulness. We can excuse or even deny our own pitiable state if we see another's condition as much worse. How, then, can this human evil be changed?

We must always remember that the other, each and every human person you encounter, Scripture tells us, is created in God's image. From the loving intent of the creator springs humankind. "Male and female God created them." Love of God and love of the other are inseparably linked. We can run off into our own hysteria and prejudice justifying the hatred of others, but by doing this we are lost, bereft and far from God. Job tells us: "For what is the hope of the godless when God cuts them off, when God takes away their lives?" (Job 27:8). "For what will it profit them if they gain the whole world but forfeit their life?" (Matthew 16:26).

When we deny the link between God and humanity we are in utmost moral, ethical and spiritual danger. *This individual is not given just as a physical body, but as a sensitive, living body belonging to an "I," an "I" that senses, thinks, feels and wills. The living body of this "I" not only fits into my phenomenal [real] world but is itself the center of orientation of such a phenomenal world. It faces this world and communicates with me.*[4]

When we accept that the other is God's handiwork and that God identifies with every human being, then ridiculing the other means ridiculing God and ourselves. We are led to see the other as almost another universe apart from us, but facing us. We see ourselves in each other because we share the same nature, uniquely expressed. We are "fearfully and wonderfully made" (Psalm 139:14).

Rabbi Abraham Heschel wrote: "As a thing man is explicable; as a person he is both a mystery and a surprise. As a thing he is finite; as a person he is inexhaustible."[5] This brother or sister in front of us, in all his or her difference becomes the only occasion for us to express our faith. We love God only to the degree that we respect these others and practice goodness toward even those who wrong us.

God has chosen, continually, to work out infinite purposes with finite tools—us. We who are created in God's image yet know the *yetzer ha-ra'*—the power and persistence of a kind of evil instinct—original sin, as we call it. We can be moved to envy and discouragement and it becomes a real struggle at times to wind up saying "But for me it is good to be near God; / I have made the Lord GOD my refuge" (Psalm 73:28). What humans are capable of is frightful and numbing. However we explain the genesis of great evil, we can never take away from the person the ultimate responsibility for their actions and decisions. In Matthew 18:6-7 we read the following from Jesus: "If any of you put a stumbling block before one of these little ones who believe in me, it would be better for you if a great millstone were fastened around your neck and you were drowned in the depth of the sea. Woe to the world because of stumbling blocks! Occasions for stumbling are bound to come, but woe to the one by whom the stumbling block comes!"

Explaining evil cannot mean explaining it away. Nor should we be lured into some anemic resignation that gives up the fight and leaves the field. The roads of history are littered with the cowardly acts of those who could have made some difference when confronted by organized hate. Love acts. It does all it can. Listen again to Rabbi Heschel: "How rarely do we face a person as a person! We are all dominated by the desire to appropriate and to own. Only a free person knows that the true meaning of existence is experienced in giving, in endowing, in meeting a person face to face, in fulfilling higher needs."[6]

Despite the apparent "dilemma" into which we are put by our human freedom, and the frightful consequences of evil, we nonetheless must persist in seeing the person in relation to God and God's creation. *When we look at the human soul in its loneliness and distress, when we witness its struggle, its fall and its rise, we are accompanied by the comforting assurance that it is in God's hands, that its path and its goal lie before the eye of the Eternal as clear as the sun, and that He has commanded His angels to watch over it.*[7]

Let me tell you a story:

Rabbi Shmuel of Nikolsburg was once asked how it is possible to love a man who does evil to him. He answered that we are told to love our fellowman as ourselves. For example, if you unintentionally strike your own body with your hand or foot, you would certainly not grow angry at your hand or foot. Likewise we must love our fellowman and not hate him even though he hurts us, as if he were indeed one of our own limbs.[8]

In this wonderful story we learn again that it is *mercy that makes us one with God; It is implanted into the creature without severing its roots from God and makes of it a "shoot on the vine."*[9] Even those who love and thirst for goodness will know the temptation and power of *yetzer ha ra*. There is no human person not in need of mercy. *We may assume that for all of us the completion of our being in glory will not only bring freedom from the cinders of our corrupted nature, but also the development of our unfulfilled potential.*[10]

When we persist in a vision of the person in relationship to God, we are inevitably drawn through our finite selves and toward the larger and more encompassing reality of eternity. *This is what those who know the inner life have experienced over time: they were drawn into their innermost self by something with a stronger pull than the entire world outside; there they experienced the breakthrough of a new, mighty, higher life; the supernatural, divine life.*[11]

But, please, think of this reality as a oneness. The seeds of divine life have been planted in all of us. God's purposes are brought to fruition in and through our ordinary lives. There are impenetrable veils separating the spheres of the finite and the divine, but there is not a radical discontinuity. Blessed be God—who is above and beyond yet present and near!

Many scholars have taught the importance of the development of the self for healthy relationship. Teresa of Avila, for example, continually advised: "Know thyself." Our emotional life is the loamy soil from which relationships are born. Think of emotions as impulses to action. *The soul perceives its own being in the stirrings of the emotions. Through the emotions, it comes to know what it is and how it is; it also grasps through them the relationship of another being to itself, and then, consequently, the significance of the inherent value of exterior things; of unfamiliar people and impersonal things.*[12] In your own day many people talk about "emotional intelligence." By this they mean the ability to recognize and name what one feels as one feels it. As I learn to do this with ease and courage I become more able to understand and relate to the other who is right in front of me. A large part of self-acceptance involves the realization of one's own failures and weaknesses. Thus, compassion is drawn from the well of repentance that necessarily follows on self-knowledge. My neighbor, this other, struggles like myself and needs love that is expressed in patience. Keep in mind: *Prayer* is the way God enters our life in terms of the person's relation to heaven. *Humility* is the way God enters our life in terms of the person's relation to the self. *Compassion* is the way God enters our lives in relationship to each other.[13] In this human-divine view of things, right relationships acknowledge the sovereignty of God, respect all persons as persons, accept the need for repentance and a change of heart, and see compassion as the highest universal expression of self-acceptance and love of the other. In this wisdom and practice you will not go wrong. Take these thoughts into a place and time of quiet and solitude and prayer.

For Reflection

- *When have you struggled to overcome a prejudice or unfair judgment? How does your faith color your perception of others?*

- *When do you notice that others are judging you? On what do you hope they base their judgment?*

Closing Prayer

Lord, help us to remember that, *for the Christian there is no stranger. Whoever is near us and needing us most is our neighbor; it does not matter whether he is related to us or not, whether he is morally worthy of our help or not, whether we like him or not. The love of Christ knows no limits. He came for sinners, not for the just. And if the love of Christ is in us, we shall do as He did and seek the lost sheep.* Amen.

Notes

[1] Michael Lerner, *Jewish Renewal: A Path to Healing and Transformation* (New York: HarperPerennial, 1995), p. 27.

[2] Edith Stein, *From a Pentecost Novena*, The Collected Works of Edith Stein (Washington, D.C.: ICS Publications, 1989).

[3] Edith Stein, *On the Problem of Empathy*, Volume 3, The Collected Works of Edith Stein (Washington, D.C.: ICS Publications, 1989), p. 110.

[4] Stein, *On the Problem of Empathy*, p. 5.

[5] Abraham Joshua Heschel, *Who Is Man?* (Stanford, Calif.: Stanford University Press, 1965), p. 28.

[6] Heschel, *Who Is Man?*, p. 61.

[7] Susanne M. Batzdorff, trans., *An Edith Stein Daybook: To Live at the Hand of God* (Springfield, Ill.: Templegate Publishers, 1994), p. 9.

[8] Samuel H. Dresner, *Prayer, Humility and Compassion* (Philadelphia: The Jewish Publication Society of America, 1957), p. 227.

[9] Stein, *On the Problem of Empathy*, p. 23.

[10] Stein, *On the Problem of Empathy*, p. 111.

[11] Stein, *On the Problem of Empathy*, p. 70.

[12] Edith Stein, *Essays on Woman*, Volume 2, The Collected Works of Edith Stein (Washington, D.S.: 1987), p. 96.

[13] Dresner, *Prayer, Humility and Compassion*, p. 183.

DAY THREE
Empathy

Coming Together in the Spirit

In *The Sun & Moon Over Assisi,* Gerard Straub tells of his encounter with a hungry homeless woman. He feels gratified that he notices her and offers a bit of help. In explaining his gratification, he quotes D.H. Lawrence's essay "We Need One Another."

> We lack peace because we are not whole. And we are not whole because we have known only a tithe of the vital relationships we might have had. We live in an age which believes in stripping away relationships.... Everything, even individuality itself, depends on relationship.... The light shines only when the circuit is completed. My individualism is really an illusion. I am part of the great whole and I can never escape.[1]

Opening Prayer

Are you the ray
That flashes down from the eternal Judge's throne
And breaks into the night of the soul
That had never known itself?
Mercifully relentlessly
It penetrates hidden folds.

Alarmed at seeing itself,
The self makes space for holy fear,
The beginning of that wisdom
That comes from on high
And anchors us firmly in the heights,
Your action,
That creates us anew:
Holy Spirit ray that penetrates everything![2]

Retreat Session Three
The Friendship That Becomes Community

Today's retreat session enlarges upon yesterday's theme. Our view of others and our propensity toward violence are directly related. When we embrace a view of the person in relationship to God and, therefore, to ourselves, violence becomes impossible; it makes no sense. Perhaps empathy begins when violence has been ruled out; or rather empathy precludes violence.

Empathy does not accept a "tyranny of the self" which always puts "I" needs before those of others. Empathy does not give way to distorted thinking that can put one group's interests above others. The empathic person "walks in the other's shoes" inasmuch as we are actually able to do so. Empathy begins in self-knowledge, reaches out in compassion to others and then goes beyond the self to a place where friendship is important and possible. Community can then become the offspring of mutual self-regard.

There is a kind of "greed of expectation" that grows

like a mushroom out of affluence. When we are surrounded with adequate shelter, plenty of food and a comfortable lifestyle, we begin to think we are entitled to them. Soon, we may begin to believe that we are entitled to other things as well, including the respect and love of others. When we believe that it is our right to have everything that it is possible to have, unrealistic expectations continue to have sway over our desires and thoughts. Then if our expectations are not met, we might react with disappointment or anger rather than the necessary self-examination that would moderate what may actually be an exaggerated self-centeredness.

Right relationships acknowledge God's sovereignty and respect all God's handiwork. Right relationships begin within the self where we see contrition as an expression of the truth about our human condition— in its woundedness and shortcomings. The need for penitence applies to all the usual, daily encounters as well as to those between nations and peoples.

Intimacy and friendship are not ours for the asking. They are not easy to achieve and are not had without patience and endurance. When we talk about empathy we are in a realm of profound ideas and feelings. Thoughts about empathy draw us immediately into a more profound consideration of the mystery of human consciousness, and to our own self-consciousness. For all its greatness, our self-consciousness is yet modest, because it is body-bound and necessarily limited. The time spent on understanding the very function we use to understand is well worth our efforts. A consideration of self-consciousness—ours and others—is not far from the recognition of freedom and of morality, and a true pursuit of holiness.

Let me quote a theologian/scientist who is a contemporary of yours. This could shed some light.

The existence of consciousness is a fact of
fundamental significance about the world in which
we live. Each of us experiences it, and only the most
skeptical of philosophers would question that we
rightly extrapolate from our individual perception
of it to the belief that its possession is shared by
other humans and, to a lesser degree by the higher
animals. The essence of consciousness is awareness
rather than mere ratiocination.[3]

This awareness is a true sense of empathy which
thrusts us back to a bold and clear realization of our own
solitude and individuality. A keen awareness of our own
interior states may be quite painful, and the admission of
vulnerability, incompleteness and imperfection is not a
comfortable awareness. Yet the more intensely aware we
are of our own thoughts and emotions, the more we are
enabled to appreciate the other. *Not through the feeling of
oneness, but through empathizing, do we experience others. The
feeling of oneness and the enrichment of our own experience
become possible through empathy.*[4] At the same time, caution
is merited so we may not be deceived. A sense of oneness
or identification is always tentative and incomplete when
it comes to the other, who, despite intimacy, inevitably
and stands as a profound, unique mystery.

A deep respect for others becomes possible from an
increased respect for oneself. Rabbi Heschel writes:

"Being human is a novelty not a mere repetition
or extension of the past, an anticipation of things
to come. Being human is a surprise, not a foregone
conclusion. A person has a capacity to create events.
Every person is a disclosure, and example of
exclusiveness."[5]

Friendship is a kind of sustained empathy that moves
us to be steadfast in our openness and positive regard
for those who have come into our lives. We may be

disappointed in our friends and need to confront each other, but we are loyal to them and to the relationship through thick and thin. Even in bad times, we are willing to wait for a new dawn of tranquility when an even deeper relationship will come to be. In friendship we are far from indifference. Indifference begets enmity and allows us to magnify our rights in some inflated outrage, while minimizing the needs of the others on whom we project our ire. The self-consciousness that so defines us and is so sacred can also lead us astray. When we cannot admit any culpability for ourselves or our social group, it becomes convenient to scapegoat others and heap upon them grossly exaggerated and distorted blame. The rise of the Nazis to power is one tragic example of this. Its aftermath of horror and death is, sadly, well known to us. Though outrage at such things is necessary it is not enough. Recounting the sins of the past must be quickly followed by real tasks for the present or the legacy of indifference and aggression will be repeated.

Love of God and neighbor can be compared to two people holding each other's hands. The fingers of the two hands are intertwined in a kind of oneness. As the two hands show how the two persons regard each other, so love of God and love of neighbor are likewise inseparable. *Hesed* refers to God's steadfast love, enduring mercy, and unshakable commitment to the covenant. *Hesed* can also be understood to refer to relationships between people. In fact, we can consider it a standard by which we measure our relationships with one another. Empathy is an expression of *hesed*. Friendship is possible even when symbols and beliefs clash and differences are boldly drawn. When dialogue can go no further toward common thinking and belief, love is always at the ready to accept the mystery of seemingly unsolvable impasses still as a true unfolding of God's will. This is not an acceptance of

injustice in large issues or small, but our enduring hope
that the One who promises justice is trustworthy.

These impasses may be events that play out noisily
on the world stage, or they may manifest as deep pain in
very ordinary, everyday events. Even in the Carmel where
I felt dearly loved, there were incidents that were hurtful.
Once I was showing the sisters pictures of my relatives
and one of them remarked, "My Lord, do they look
Jewish!"[6] I am sure that each of us can recall words and
sentiments that were deeply hurtful. Such thoughtlessness
challenges us in our humanity to keep our balance in
anger and disappointment. As ever, God's enduring love
is our hope and our strength. We cannot always transcend
the human limitations imposed on us by time, space,
culture, biology and history. In God, however, all these
realities are always overcome. *It has always been far from
me to think that God's mercy allows itself to be circumscribed
by the visible church's boundaries. God is truth. All who seek
truth seek God, whether this is clear to them or not.*[7]

As our empathy expresses God's *hesed*, so community
becomes possible as its outgrowth. Like ourselves, our
communities are never perfect. This realization can
be painful, frustrating and deeply disappointing. But
"success" is not necessarily to be found in the external
accomplishments of our communities, but in an enduring
commitment to mutual self-regard. Sometimes our
respect for the other can only be a patient silence and
acknowledgment of the very real differences between us.
God does not call us always to reach agreement, but to
love one another regardless of our circumstances.

For Reflection

- *When have you developed a close relationship with a person whom you did not initially like? What changed— the individual or your own perceptions?*

- *How can you express "love of neighbor" where it is most needed in your life?*

- *Are there friends with whom you have lost contact over the years? Try calling or sending a note to catch up.*

Closing Prayer

The law of the Lord rises opposite all the interplay of likes and dislikes: You shall love your neighbor as yourself. That is valid—no ifs and buts. The "neighbor" is not someone I like. My neighbor is anyone who comes near me, without exception.[8] Lord, help us to remember the needs of our neighbors and our obligation to love them. Help us to discover the holiness in our friendships and in ourselves. Amen.

Notes

[1] Gerard Thomas Straub, *The Sun and Moon Over Assisi: A Personal Encounter With Francis and Clare* (Cincinnati: St. Anthony Messenger Press, 2000), p. 85.

[2] Edith Stein, *From a Pentecost Novena, The Collected Works of Edith Stein* (Washington, D.C.: ICS Publications, 1989).

[3] John C. Polkinghorne, *The Faith of a Physicist* (Minneapolis: Fortress Press, 1996), p. 11.

[4] Edith Stein, *On the Problem of Empathy*, Volume 3, *The Collected Works of Edith Stein* (Washington, D.C.: ICS Publications, 1989), p. 18.

[5] Samuel H. Dresner, *I Asked for Wonder: A Spiritual Anthology of Abraham Joshua Heschel* (New York: Crossroads, 1998), p. 48.

[6] Susanne M. Batzdorff, *Aunt Edith: The Jewish Heritage of a Catholic Saint* (Springfield, Ill.: Templegate Publishers, 1998), pp. 128-129. Susanne writes of this incident not as an opportunity for humility, as someone else had commented, but as an occasion of deep hurt for Edith. Edith's response to this remark is recorded nowhere.

[7] Edith Stein, *Self-Portrait in Letters*, trans., Sr. Josephine Koeppel, O.C.D. (Washington, D.C.: ICS Publications, 1993), p. 272. Edith writes this to Sr. Adelgundis in relation to Edmund Husserl.

[8] Susanne M. Batzdorff, trans., *An Edith Stein Daybook: To Live at the Hand of God* (Springfield, Ill.: Templegate Publishers, 1994), p. 70.

Day Four
Prayer

"To stand before the face of the living God—
that is our vocation."[1]

Coming Together in the Spirit

The Baal Shem Tov told this parable about prayer:

There was once a king who was very wise, and by
magic which deceived the eyes of the beholder,
he made imaginary walls and towers and gates to
surround his palace. He also gave a command that
those who wanted to see him must enter through
the gates and towers. He further ordered that at
each gate riches from his treasuries be given away.

Now there were those who came to the first gate,
received money and, being satisfied, went back
home. There were those who [were deterred by the
imposing walls and barriers, or who lost their way
in all the various gates and walls]. No one was able
to enter and see the king, until the king's beloved
son came—and he was determined to exert all his
efforts to see his father, the king, without being
deterred by good or bad. And [due to this firm
determination and unrelenting desire] he saw that
there was no barrier at all between himself and his
father, for it was all just a magical illusion.[2]

Opening Prayer

> Are you the spirit's fullness and the power
> By which the Lamb releases the seal
> Of God's eternal decree?
> Driven by you
> The messengers of judgement ride through
>   the world
> And separate with a sharp sword
> The kingdom of light from the kingdom of night.
> Then heaven becomes new and new the earth,
> And all finds its proper place
> Through your breath:
> Holy Spirit victorious power![3]

RETREAT SESSION FOUR
The Craft of Prayer

Our time together on this retreat is for deep consideration of our lives in prayer with God. Today we will turn more of a spotlight on just a few aspects of that life. Perhaps we could compare it to a boat moored in the water. This tiny ship (prayer) aids us in traveling on the bay of life. Each day we take care to see that it is fit to take us out onto the waters of God's work and purposes. As we would maintain our watercraft, so should we pay consistent attention to prayer in our lives. The treasures of prayer are for the whole people of God. Reflectiveness and a contemplative spirit can be ours in some way in any circumstance. An example of this is our father Elijah as recorded in 1 Kings 19. The prophet was in great danger after his confrontation with the prophets of Baal.

He fled for his life. Elijah arrived at Horeb, called Sinai in the Judahite literature. The word of the Lord came to him.

> "Go out and stand on the mountain before the Lord, for the Lord is about to pass by." Now there was a great wind, so strong that it was splitting mountains and breaking rocks in pieces before the Lord, but the Lord was not in the wind; and after the wind an earthquake, but the Lord was not in the earthquake; and after the earthquake a fire, but the Lord was not in the fire; and after the fire *a sound of sheer silence.* When Elijah heard it, he wrapped his face in his mantle and went out and stood at the entrance of the cave. (1 Kings 19:11-13)

Out of the *sheer silence* came direction for Elijah. Elijah is a patron of Carmel and an example of prayer for all of us. He expected the Lord to speak to him and guide him. Our commitment to prayer begins in the same kind of humility and trust that covers all aspects of our existence. We come to realize that it is we who need to accommodate to God's purposes. God is not bound to yield to ours. We remember that "Our knowledge is piecemeal. When our will and action build on it alone, they cannot achieve a perfect structure. Nor can that knowledge, because it does not have complete power over the self and often collapses before reaching the goal. And so this inner shaping power that is in bondage strains toward a light that will guide more surely, and a power that will free it and give it space. This is the light and power of divine grace."[4]

God is keeper of the boat and the waters. Prayer at all times and in all climates involves seeking God's guidance for each tiny segment of the journey. We are not alone nor do we, by great effort, agonize to figure out God's will. Interiority may begin in the hard and humbling school of self-knowledge, but it liberates, finally, in realizations of love and care. *God knows every human soul from eternity, with every secret of its being and every lapping of the waves of its life.*[5] We are cradled in that knowledge. It is our place of wholeness. Only in the embrace of God's total graciousness do we truly come to fulfillment. *One cannot lift one's eyes to God without being aware of one's own insignificance. Awareness of God and of the self are mutually supportive. Through self-awareness we come closer to God. Therefore it is never superfluous.*[6]

We could spend our whole retreat discussing prayer. It is so multi-faceted. Perhaps it will be helpful to think about prayer in the following ways: how prayer enhances our relationships; how even in darkness it bears fruit; how it invites us to solitude and newer depths of prayer; and how it draws us toward transformation and union with God.

Prayer enhances relationship

My entrance into Carmel was a great hardship for my mother. She believed strongly in her Jewish faith. She also imagined terrible things about convents and nuns. And I know she reproached herself for not being more diligent in my early religious formation. Her faith was so strong and was always an inspiration to me, yet I could not convince her that this was so. Our last days together were difficult ones. *Everything remained in all its starkness and incomprehensibility, and I was able to leave (her) only by placing a firm confidence in God's grace and the strength of our prayer. That my mother, too, has faith, and finally, that she still has great inner strength made it a little easier.*[7]

Each of us is filled with shadows; misunderstandings and painful moments are characteristic of all relationships. In patient acceptance of our mutual weakness and fragility we draw near to God's love for humankind and partake of it. What we cannot now fathom and understand makes perfect sense in God's providential care. Prayer

becomes a dwelling place in that care. The difficulties
we have with each other are not final when we take into
consideration where every soul is headed. *The story of
souls is hidden deep in God's heart. And what we sometimes
think we understand of our own soul is, after all, always just
a fleeting reflection of that which remains God's secret until
the day when all is revealed.*[8] The present does not often
yield an abundance of clarity. But clear understanding
is not always necessary to love and relationship.

Prayer and the fruit of darkness

All my life I had prided myself on being German,
and had nursed German soldiers during the Great War.
Now I was being declared a non-person as I prepared to
go to the Echt Carmel in Holland where all thought my
safety could be assured. My relatives were living in fear of
their lives as National Socialism began its comprehensive
attack on Jews and others distasteful to them. It was a
time of such great darkness and pain! The Carmelites at
Cologne had plans to open a monastery in Breslau and
I immediately requested to be assigned to it so that I
might be closer to my mother. I thought that would be
a consolation to her. None of this would come to be,
however. All around me was darkness. Mine were the
words of the Psalmist:

> My tears have been my food
>   day and night....
> I say to God, my rock,
>   "Why have you forgotten me?
> Why must I walk about mournfully
>   Because the enemy oppresses me?"
>   (Psalm 42:3, 9)

There are times when the mystery of God's love is
dreadful! Sorrow can appear to drown us.

> Deep calls to deep,
>   At the thunder of your cataracts;
> All your waves and your billows
>   Have gone over me. (Psalm 42:7)

Great anguish is a part of life and likewise of prayer. The way out is the way through. What sustains us in times of joy, likewise nourishes the soul in darkness.

> Why are you cast down, O my soul,
>   and why are you disquieted within me?
> Hope in God; for I shall again praise him,
>   my help and my God. (Psalm 42:11)

The fruit of darkness is our hope. It grows through that prayer which stands firm in the storm that it cannot stop or change. What we discover is that the fruit of darkness is the power of love manifested in the cross that casts its shadow over all the world. Standing in our places of darkness is standing with Christ and with all those who await the victory of goodness and make it evident in their efforts for goodness despite any circumstance.

Prayer and solitude

You may be surprised to learn that I had more solitude outside of Carmel than within it![9] As much as I loved work and people, I also cherished solitary prayer in those years before I came to the contemplative life. Life in Carmel allowed me two hours for solitary time with the Lord each day. Far from being an odious duty, it was my joy! I found there a fullness that I had always lacked. *The confidence that something of our peace and our silence flows out into the world, and supports those who are still on pilgrimage, is the only thing that can reassure me when I consider that I, rather than so many other worthy ones, have been called into this wonderful security.*[10] Certainly, all are not called to

Carmel or to religious orders. There is no reason, however, to deny ourselves the consolations of solitude and prayer. In a practical vein, we all fill our days with many activities. Sometimes one hears that people need things to do to "pass the time." Surely, then, we can carve out some time for the Lord's special presence in the Eucharist. "He knows we need his personal nearness. He is not present for his own sake but for ours; it is his delight to be with us."[11] What we once thought a time of boredom can become an oasis of meaning. Solitude and even loneliness have their own truths to impart and beauties to share. I always loved the Breviary which, in Carmel, we used daily. Many adaptations have been made of this "Prayer of the Church" for different persons and circumstances. All of these open up to you the riches of the Psalms and a fuller acquaintance with the Scriptures. Once you realize that these have direct and real applicability to your own circumstances, you will find that great fruitfulness comes from the most modest efforts. I want to encourage you in this! Pick a time and a place each day for time alone in prayer with God.

Prayer and union

There is a beautiful painting of the Transfiguration of Christ by Fra Angelico. He shows Peter, James and John overcome with awe. Jesus stands on a huge rock in dazzling white robes. He also painted the heads of Moses and Elijah who each are present in this moment of glorification. Jesus' arms are straight out from his body in a cruciform. It strikes one immediately. When you return to the Scripture accounts (Matthew 17:1-9, Mark 9:2-8, Luke 9:28-36) you must note that each account of Jesus' transfiguration is preceded by this:

From that time on, Jesus began to show his disciples

that he must go to Jerusalem and undergo great
suffering at the hands of the elders and chief priests
and scribes, and be killed, and on the third day
be raised. And Peter took him aside and began to
rebuke him, saying, "God forbid it, Lord! This must
never happen to you." But he turned and said to
Peter, "Get behind me, Satan! You are a stumbling
block to me; for you are setting your mind not on
divine things but on human things" (Matthew 16:
21-23).

Even Jesus' closest followers recoiled at their Lord's
mention of suffering and death. Yet Peter learned this
lesson well over time. Later in his life he writes:

His divine power has given us everything needed
for life and godliness, through the knowledge of
him who called us by his own glory and goodness....
[Y]ou must make every effort to support your faith
with goodness, and goodness with knowledge,
and knowledge with self-control, and self-control
with endurance, and endurance with godliness,
and godliness with mutual affection, and mutual
affection with love.... For we did not follow cleverly
devised myths when we made known to you the
power and coming of our Lord Jesus Christ, but we
had been eyewitnesses of his majesty. (2 Peter 1:3,
5-7, 16)

Our union with God is through Christ in the power of
the Resurrection. We may wish to conspire with Peter (in
Matthew 16:22) and promote a Christ without suffering,
but these are mere human ways not those of God. We
have all fallen short of the glory of God, and we have
done that in an arrogance, however small, that purports
to know more than God does about the way one's life is
to go, and the manner in which God's purposes will be
accomplished. To rest in God is to rest in the strength that

God offers for goodness, endurance, self-control, mutual affection and love. Our union with God is not found in moments of ecstasy, but in our response to the darkness that may surround our prayer, our relationships, our circumstances and our striving.

For Reflection

- *What new realization is God calling you to in your life of prayer?*

- *How will tomorrow be different than today for you when you go to prayer?*

- *How in your life can you "stand before the living God" for others in prayer?*

- *How can you allow the sheer silence of listening into your life?*

Closing Prayer

The call to union with God is a call to eternal life. By nature the human soul as a purely spiritual entity is not mortal. Besides, as a spiritual personal entity it is capable of a supernatural intensification of life, and faith teaches us that God wishes to give the soul eternal life, that is an eternal share in His life.[10]

Notes

[1] Edith Stein, *The Hidden Life: Essays, Meditations, Spiritual Texts*, Volume 4, *The Collected Works of Edith Stein* (Washington, D.C.: ICS Publications, 1992), p. 1.

[2] Yitzhak Buxbaum *Jewish Spiritual Practices* (Northvale, N.J.: Jason Aronson, Inc.), pp. 124-125.

[3] Edith Stein, *From a Pentecost Novena, The Collected Works of Edith Stein* (Washington, D.C.: ICS Publications, 1989).

[4] Stein, *The Hidden Life*, p. 28.

[5] Susanne M. Batzdorff, trans., *An Edith Stein Daybook: To Live at the Hand of God* (Springfield, Ill.: Templegate Publishers, 1994), p. 19.

[6] Batzdorff, *An Edith Stein Daybook*, p. 21.

[7] Edith Stein, *Self-Portrait in Letters*, trans., Sr. Josephine Koeppel, O.C.D. (Washington, D.C.: ICS Publications, 1993), p. 163.

[8] Stein, *Self-Portrait in Letters*, p. 199. Edith mentions the Reverend Konrad Swind in a 1935 letter.

[9] Stein, *Self-Portrait in Letters*, p. 197, in a letter to Gertrud Von Le Fort.

[10] Stein, *Self-Portrait in Letters*, p. 146. Edith herself uses this phrase at the close of a letter to Sr. Callista Kopf, O.P., a friend of hers.

[11] Stein, *Self-Portrait in Letters*, p. 141, in a letter to Sister Maria Elisabeth, O.C.D.

DAY FIVE
The Eucharist

"For I received from the Lord what I also handed on to you, that the Lord Jesus, on the night when he was betrayed, took a loaf of bread, and, when he had given thanks, he broke it and said, 'This is my body that is for you. Do this in remembrance of me.' In the same way he took the cup also, after supper, saying, 'This cup is the new covenant in my blood. Do this, as often as you drink it, in remembrance of me. For as often as you eat this bread and drink the cup, you proclaim the Lord's death until he comes.'"
—1 Corinthians 11:23-25

Coming Together in the Spirit

In her *Essays on Woman*, Edith Stein wrote memorably about her experience of Eucharist:

Only in daily, confidential relationship with the Lord in the tabernacle can one forget self, become free of all one's own wishes and pretentions, and have a heart open to all the needs and wants of others. Whoever seeks to consult with the Eucharistic God in all her concerns, whoever lets herself be purified by the sanctifying power coming from the sacrifice at the altar, offering herself to the Lord in this sacrifice, whoever receives the Lord in her soul's innermost depth in Holy communion

cannot but be drawn ever more deeply and
powerfully into the flow of divine life, incorporated
into the Mystical Body of Christ, her heart converted
to the likeness of the divine heart.[1]

Opening Prayer

Are you the master who builds the
    eternal cathedral,
Which towers from the earth through
    the heavens?
Animated by you, the columns are
    raised high
And stand immovably firm.
Marked with the eternal name of God,
They stretch up to the light,
Bearing the dome,
Which crowns the holy cathedral,
Your work that encircles the world:
Holy Spirit God's molding hand![2]

RETREAT SESSION FIVE

The Mystery of Christ With Us

We have spent the last two sessions considering
prayer, empathy and friendship. We know that these are
both expressions of relationship and presence. With those
wonderful realizations in mind, we turn to the mystery
of Christ still with us. Can we even count the times we
have heard and prayed these words that Paul hands on to
us? How usual they have become! What is it that we do?

What is it that we bring to mind when we gather, give thanks and remember? Paul notes that he is handing on what he received. He writes in the fifth decade of the first century of the Common Era and is transmitting a tradition that was in existence before his own knowledge and acceptance of Jesus. The early first century believers attended Temple frequently, perhaps even daily and they "broke the bread" in their homes (see Acts 2:46). Their remembrance at the sacred meal was, at that time, in continuity with their hopes for Israel. They waited for God's intervention to deliver them. Theirs was an eschatological hope. They looked to the future from an always expectant and hopeful present. Luke writes: "He said to them, 'I have eagerly desired to eat this Passover with you before I suffer; for I tell you, I will not eat it until it is fulfilled in the kingdom of God'" (Luke 22: 15-16; see also Matthew 26:29, and Mark 14:25). *Do this in remembrance of me.* Jesus points us to the future in a continuum of sacrifice, presence, mission and fulfillment. What begins at a certain point in time is a pledge and a promise of what is yet to come.

The Gospels tell us that Christ prayed the way a devout Jew faithful to the law prayed. Just as he made pilgrimages to Jerusalem at the prescribed times with his parents as a child, so he later journeyed to the temple to celebrate the high feasts there with his disciples. Surely he sang with holy enthusiasm along with his people the exultant hymns in which the pilgrim's joyous anticipation streamed forth: "I rejoiced when I heard them say: Let us go to God's house" (Psalm 122:1). From his Last Supper with his disciples we know that Jesus said the old blessings over bread, wine, and the fruits of the earth, as they pray to this day. So he fulfilled one of the most sacred religious duties: the ceremonial Passover seder to commemorate deliverance from slavery in Egypt.[3]

Jesus Our Deliverance

Both Luke and Paul mention in their accounts that the cups of remembrance which Jesus drinks speak of deliverance and call to mind God's intervention in bringing the Israelites out of Egypt (See Luke 22:20 and 1 Corinthians 11:25). A sacred meal with Kiddush (blessing) cups of wine, brings us into God's presence where time and eternity meet. What God has done and what God will do are mysteriously joined. Time is sanctified. The prayers and the partaking of the cups raise us into a triumphant hope that finds its comfort in the surety of God's promises. God who brought the Israelites out of slavery will bring us to the total fulfillment of the realm of lasting peace and justice. The sorrow and suffering of the present moment do not invalidate what the Holy One is accomplishing. Jesus Our Deliverance prays thus as he leaves the upper room and moves toward his suffering and death.

We can imagine ourselves walking with Jesus and praying the glorious Hallell (Psalms 113-118) that he chanted with his followers on that sacred night. We recall that the Lord helps the humble.

> He raises the poor from the dust,
>   and lifts the needy from the ash heap.....
> He gives a barren woman a home... (Psalm 113:7, 9).

In Psalm 114 we recall God's great work in creating the nation of Israel:

> Judah became God's sanctuary,
>   Israel his dominion. (Psalm 114:2)

Our souls flood with gratitude and humility at God's mighty deeds.

> Not to us, O LORD, not to us, but to your name give glory,
>   for the sake of your steadfast love and your
>   faithfulness. (Psalm 115:1)

The Psalmist gathers up the collective experience of God's people in Psalm 116:

> I love the LORD, because he has heard
>> my voice and my supplications. (Psalm 116:1)

We recount the formidable struggles that the people have endured:

> The snares of death encompassed me;...
> I suffered distress and anguish....
> I kept my faith, even when I said,
>> "I am greatly afflicted";...
> What shall I return to the LORD
>> for all this bounty to me?
> I will lift up the cup of salvation
>> and call on the name of the LORD.
>> (Psalm 116:3, 10, 12-13)

The Lord Jesus knew that the cups he lifted were full of hope. Yet his fear was real and the impending suffering frightful.

> The Lord is on my side to help me;
>> I shall look in triumph on those who hate me....
> They surrounded me like bees;
>> they blazed like a fire of thorns;...
> I was pushed hard, so that I was falling,
>> but the LORD helped me. (Psalm 118:7, 12, 13)

Jesus our deliverance becomes a blessing cup. In the face of suffering and death he calls to mind God's goodness and magnificence. We bring to mind how God answers Job:

> Is it by your wisdom that the hawk soars,
>> and spreads its wings toward the south?
> Is it at your command that the eagle mounts up
>> and makes its nest on high? (Job 39:26-27)

Job gets no explanation specific to his suffering save the

glory and power of the Almighty One whose Wisdom permeates creation. In utter trust of God Job accepts both prosperity and suffering. Jesus blesses. He is full of gratitude. He lifts up the cup of his life, suffering, death and resurrection and bids us do likewise. *Do this in remembrance of me.* What is it, then, that we do in remembrance? We live in Thanksgiving despite present evil. Recall Paul's words "I am convinced that neither death,...nor present things, nor future things...nor any other creature will be able to separate us from the love of God in Christ Jesus our Lord" (Romans 8:38-39). In the act of remembrance we partake of Jesus' fidelity. In remembrance we are joined to him and to each other and to God's purposes being mysteriously but surely realized in human history, in our own individual histories and that of others. Our deliverance comes through a lived remembrance united to the utter trust of Jesus Our Wisdom. The journey is not yet ended, so we pass on the message with our blood. We give all that there is to give. "Do this in remembrance of me."

Jesus our Servant Lord

John the evangelist gives no account of the institution of the Eucharist. His Last Supper account is part of what many call "The Book of Glory" beginning at Chapter 13 in John's narrative. Jesus finishes his public ministry then gathers with his disciples and takes on the servant's role of washing the feet of those at the dinner. All this takes place surrounded by the bitter sorrow of impending betrayal. Jesus knows that his hour has come. John records Jesus saying that God's commandment is eternal life (John 12:50). Thus, the Lord speaks and acts out of profound purpose, union and obedience.

When Jesus comes to wash Peter's feet Peter resists:

"Peter said to him, 'You will never wash my feet.' Jesus answered, 'Unless I wash you, you have no share with me.'" This washing that Jesus enjoins points to the saving waters of Baptism.

When we enter into Christ's life through the ritual of Baptism, we embrace the servanthood of Christ. We have been bought at a great price, and find ourselves humbled and eager at the reality and immensity of the Lord's fidelity and self-sacrifice. In our acceptance of Baptism is our acceptance of the Suffering Servant's way. We learn to proclaim with Peter who, rather than be turned away by Jesus, pleads: "Lord, not my feet only but also my hands and my head!" Peter's impetuosity teaches us that God asks for the full gift of ourselves. *Whoever surrenders unconditionally to the Lord will be chosen by him as an instrument in building the Kingdom.*[4]

What we do in authentic remembrance far exceeds intellectual assent. We kneel down in front of others, and from the basin of our life's work, soothe the hearts of others in whatever needs may arise at the time and in the circumstances. Our following of Christ is both practical and profound.

"Do this in remembrance of me." Take my presence to every encounter with human misery. Be my mercy. "I appeal to you, therefore, brothers and sisters, by the mercies of God, to present your bodies as a living sacrifice, holy and acceptable to God, which is your spiritual worship" (Romans 12:1-2). *All authentic prayer is prayer of the church. Through every sincere prayer something happens in the church, and it is the church itself that is praying therein, for it is the Holy Spirit living in the church that intercedes for every individual soul "with sighs too deep for words" (Romans 8:26). This is exactly what "authentic" prayer is, for "no one can say Jesus is Lord except by the Holy Spirit" (1 Corinthians 12:3). What could the prayer of the church be, if not great lovers giving themselves to God who is love!*[5]

When Jesus takes the basin and the towel, glory is wed to humble and ordinary deeds. And so our worship 'in spirit and in truth' is woven into the texture of our lives. Individual deeds complement public endeavors. Life, prayer and loving become one. In our most private moments we are the most transparent. However obscure or hidden our prayer we are nonetheless called to be moral beacons. Our very thoughts are like speeches in God's eyes and the eyes of others.

For Reflection

- *What is your experience of Eucharist?*

- *How can you bring the presence of Christ to those people and place that most need it?*

- *In what ways do your own earthly concerns mask the glory of God within you? How can you use this insight to focus on what is truly important?*

Closing Prayer

For the feast of Corpus Christi in 1935, Sister Teresa Benedicta prepared a poem for Sister Maria who took her vows on this date. Edith adorned the cover of the booklet with a heart surrounded by thorns inside a triangle reminding us of the Trinity. We read these verses in profound gratitude for the sacrificial love of Jesus made present to us over and over again. We also recall and admire Edith Stein's courage throughout her own Calvary. "He who eats my flesh and drinks my blood

lives in me and I live in him. As I, who am sent by
the living Father myself draw life from the Father. So
whoever eats me will draw life from me" (John 6: 56-57).

I Shall Stay With You...

Your throne is at the Lord's right hand
Within the realm of His eternal glory
God's word from when the world began.

For where you are, there also are your dear ones.
And heaven is my glorious fatherland,
With you I share the father's throne.

The inmost chamber of the human soul
Is favorite dwelling to the Trinity,
His heavenly throne right here on earth.

Within the heart of Jesus pierced with lances,
The realms of heaven and earth become united.
And here we find the spring of life itself.

Each morn you come to me as early Mass,
Your flesh and blood become my food and drink;
And wonders are accomplished.

Your body permeates mine mysteriously,
I feel your soul becoming one with mine:
I am no longer what I used to be.

You come and go, but still the seed remains
Which you have sown for future splendor,
Hid in the body made from dust.

A heavenly radiance lingers in the soul,
And deeply shines a light within the eye,
A vibrant music in the voice.

The tie remains connecting heart to heart,

The stream of life which wells from Yours and gives
Life to each limb.

How wondrous are the marvels of your love,
We are amazed, we stammer and grow dumb,
For word and spirit fail us.[6]

Notes

[1] Edith Stein, *Essays on Woman*, Volume 2, *The Collected Works of Edith Stein* (Washington, D.C.: ICS Publications, 1987), p. 55.

[2] Edith Stein, *From a Pentecost Novena*, *The Collected Works of Edith Stein* (Washington, D.C.: ICS Publications, 1989).

[3] Edith Stein, *The Hidden Life: Essays, Meditations, Spiritual Texts*, Volume 4, *The Collected Works of Edith Stein* (Washington, D.C.: ICS Publications, 1992), p. 7.

[4] Stein, *The Hidden Life*, pp. 14-15.

[5] Stein, *The Hidden Life*, p. 15.

[6] Susanne M. Batzdorff, *Edith Stein, Selected Writings: With Comments, Reminiscences and Translations of her Prayers and Poems by her Niece* (Springfield, Ill.: Templegate Publishers, 1990), pp. 49-51.

DAY SIX
The Sabbath

*"God is truth. Those who seek truth, seek God,
whether they know it or not."*[1]

Coming Together in the Spirit

In her final letter, dated August 6, 1942, Edith Stein,
Sister Teresa Benedicta a Cruce asked Mother Superior
Ambrosia Engelmann to send her two blankets, towels
and a wash cloth. She mentions that her sister Rosa does
not have a toothbrush. She had managed to pass this
letter[2] at the Schifferstadt railway station early on August
7. A woman in "dark clothing" identified herself as
Edith Stein (she had acquaintances in that city) and left
a message either orally or perhaps in writing: "We are
traveling east." From the little we know Edith remained
hopeful right up to the end. P. O. van Kempen was one
of the last to see Edith and Rosa alive in the transition
camp of Westerbork, Holland. He writes:

> While she told their experiences, we both smoked
> cigarettes. (He and Pierre Cuypers). To lighten
> the tension a little, we jokingly presented Sister
> Benedicta with a cigarette as well. She, too, laughed
> about that and told us that, formerly, in her student
> days, she had certainly smoked cigarettes and also
> danced. Sister Benedicta was completely calm and
> self-controlled. One could not detect any trace of

fear in her about the uncertain future. Calmly and in complete surrender she had placed her life into the sure hand of God. In her clear eyes shone the glow of a holy Carmelite, who related events in a gentle voice but said nothing about her personal experiences. Rosa Stein also said that she was all right. She found much support in the example of her sister Edith.[3]

Edith and Rosa were killed three days later in Auschwitz.

Opening Prayer

Are you the one who created the unclouded
    mirror
Next to the Almighty's throne,
Like a crystal sea,
In which Divinity lovingly looks at itself?
You bend over the fairest work of your creation,
And radiantly your own gaze
Is illumined in return.
And of all creatures the pure beauty
Is joined in one in the dear form
Of the Virgin, your immaculate bride:
Holy Spirit Creator of all![4]

RETREAT SESSION SIX
Lived Truth

You may wonder how the Sabbath and lived truth are related and why I have chosen to consider them together. I hope that this will become evident and prove to be spiritually helpful. Much of my life, as you know, was spent in the pursuit of truth through philosophy. I remember those years and friendships with great fondness, and marvel how all along the way God was leading me in a most unique fashion, step by step. My own twists and turns have taught me that the significance and truth in our lives become evident only through experience. Each day is its own evidence of God's presence and care. No moment is lost, even if it is later regretted. God who loves us so, fashions all the threads of our struggling into a beautiful tapestry full of goodness. *Living at God's hand is the truth I was led to. I rested in it and found there all that was meaningful.* Truth is discovered in each moment of living, breathing and acting. Truth is both profound and pragmatic. Let's take a look at Luke's account of the beginning of Jesus' mission. We read:

> When he came to Nazareth, where he had been brought up, he went to the synagogue on the Sabbath day, as was his custom. He stood up to read, and the scroll of the prophet Isaiah was given to him. He unrolled the scroll and found the place where it was written: "The Spirit of the Lord is upon me, because he has anointed me to bring good news to the poor. He has sent me to proclaim release to the captives and recovery of sight to the blind, to let the oppressed go free, to proclaim the year of the Lord's favor." (Luke 4: 16-19)

Luke tells us that Jesus proclaims his deepest purpose and meaning on the Sabbath, in the synagogue to the assembly. These are the most ordinary circumstances for a Jewish man. The *chazzan* or attendant of the synagogue hands Jesus the scroll. He reads from Isaiah, chapter 61, and reveals God's extraordinary plan. In its original context in what is sometimes called Third Isaiah, there are transcendent elements of God's care being presented.

Most likely the passage is written in 530 to 510 B.C. or later. The restoration under King Cyrus has taken place and the prophet Isaiah ponders the mission of the Jewish people for helping to redeem the whole world. There are proclamations of the universality of the covenant mission in chapter 61. The prophet writes that "their descendants shall be known among the nations" and "the Lord God will cause righteousness and praise to spring up before all the nations."

Jesus frames his mission with these words of Isaiah. In Luke 4:19 he reads that it is time "to proclaim the year of the Lord's favor." We know that John the Baptist began his ministry in a Sabbatical year. Jesus extends this and inaugurates his mission out of sabbatical sensibilities. Jubilee time honors the need of the earth to rest and lie fallow. The needs of people to pause from toil are honored as well. In resting from labor and care, the believer finds rest in God. And in Jesus' own need for intimacy with God, we learn of our own deepest need for relationship with and in God. All human bonds become sacred as they blossom out of the divine will and plan for us.

Let me tell you another story that is another way of seeing the meaning of Jesus' lived Sabbatical truth.

> On the eve of the Day of Atonement, when the time had come to chant the Kol Nidre prayer, all the Hasidim of Rabbi Moshe Leib of Sassov were gathered together in the House of Prayer waiting for the rabbi. But time passed and he did not come. They all wondered what important matter was delaying him on this holy day. Then one of the women of the congregation said to herself: "I guess it will be a while before they begin and my child is alone in the house. I'll just run home and look after him to make sure he hasn't awakened. I can be back in a few minutes." She ran home and listened at the

door. Everything was quiet. Softly she turned the
knob and put her head into the room—and there
stood the rabbi holding her child in his arms. On his
way to the House of Prayer, he had heard the child
crying and had played with it and sung to it until it
fell asleep.[5]

This story reminds us that the Sabbath is for people; that
human needs, however unexpectedly they appear, may
cause us, by way of exception, to interrupt our prayer
time with God. Compassion and prayer are the two hands
we raise together in praise of God. One may sometimes
have to bow to the other, but they are never really in
opposition.

We honor God's will and enflesh God's favor in the
way we treat one another. The Rabbi knew that God would
be praised and honored in both the Kol Nidre prayer and
in the care of the infant. The very same God whom we
praise in worship is reflected in the merest creature. The
holy ones see this clearly and easily. When we love the
Sabbath, when we love resting in God, we have passed
beyond a rule-bound interpretation of religion to a lived
faith—a lived truth. When we love the Sabbath, we honor
the need to cease and desist from feverish toil. This rest
enables our bodies and minds to see our real needs as
well as the real needs of others. This knowledge humbles
us and teaches us to honor ourselves and our neighbors
as well as our human limitations will permit.

I mentioned before that the teaching on the Sabbath is
both profound and pragmatic. Let me explain. In human
relationships the term *differentiation* means the ability to
maintain and comfort oneself in the face of disapproval
and rejection from others. This differentiating capacity of
ours needs time, quiet and reflection. We come to it slowly
and in the midst of life's daily struggles and sufferings.
Sabbath recognizes the human need to pause and reflect

in order to be differentiating, self-transcendent and free. Our very real and practical need for rest enables us to find God's profundity.

Jesus himself spent long hours in solitude and prayer pondering God's purposes, seeking God's strength and God's will. To live the truth that comes from God; to be the lived truth that is Jesus, we come to realize that resting in God is absolutely essential. Living in honor of the Sabbath is living at God's hand. Without the Sabbath every other concern gobbles up our living. The presence of God in us, which is eternity itself, becomes obscured, blotted out and forgotten. The enjoined reflection of Sabbath is also a benefit to all creatures and to the earth itself. We recognize this rhythm of work and rest in our very bodies. We need to work but also to sleep. Animals and the earth itself find their fullness in a rhythm of work and repose.

What are we to say of the Sabbath in a world of ceaseless and often tormented endeavor? Do we truly temper the urge to fill time and space with our projects? Could it not be said that often we are preoccupied with "having" as opposed to "being"? This acquisitiveness is not just for material things but for more subtle possessions like control and prestige, importance, respect.

A wise and venerable Jewish philosopher writes: "There is a realm of time where the goal is not to have but to be, not to own but to give, not to control but to share, not to subdue but to be in accord," and, "On the Sabbath we especially care for the seed of eternity planted in the soul."[6] Who is this Lord of the Sabbath for us? What does he promise and what does he require? In Matthew 11:28-30 we read:

> Come to me, all you that are weary and are carrying heavy burdens, and I will give you rest. Take my yoke upon you, and learn from me; for I am gentle

and humble in heart, and you will find rest for your souls. For my yoke is easy and my burden is light.

Only Matthew's gospel has these words and they come after Jesus has given thanks to the Father for all the lowly souls who, like children, have accepted him in the giving up of all care. When we rest in Jesus we become part of his intimacy with God the All-loving with whom the Lord is totally One. What our Lord of the Sabbath requires is our total trust, the abandonment of all worry despite the hardships with which we are faced.

For Reflection

- *How do you observe the Sabbath? Do you think of it as a burdensome requirement or a welcome respite?*

- *When do you find yourself conscious of the "truth" of your life? How do you live that truth each day?*

- *How does a time of rest each week help you to gain perspective on the rest of your time?*

Closing Prayer

God does all things at the right time. Whatever he does is not outside of time but rather at the most opportune moment and comes at the right time for me.[7] Strengthen us, Loving Lord of the Sabbath to place our trust in you and rest in you. Help us in life and in death to cling to you, your love and your promise. You are our Way, our Life and our truth. Amen.

Notes

[1] Edith Stein, *Self-Portrait in Letters*, trans., Sr. Josephine Koeppel, O.C.D. (Washington, D.C.: ICS Publications, 1993), p. 272.

[2] Stein, *Self-Portrait in Letters*, p. 353.

[3] Waltraud Herbstrith, O.C.D. ed. *Never Forget: Christian and Jewish Perspectives on Edith Stein* (Washington, D.C.: 1998), p. 274.

[4] Edith Stein, *From a Pentecost Novena, The Collected Works of Edith Stein* (Washington, D.C.: ICS Publications, 1989.

[5] Samuel H. Dresner, *Prayer, Humility and Compassion* (Philadelphia: The Jewish Publication Society of America, 1957), pp. 221-222.

[6] Abraham Heschel, *The Sabbath, Its Meaning for Modern Man* (New York: Farrar, Straus and Giroux, 1998), pp. 3, 13.

[7] Stein, *Self-Portrait in Letters*, p. 245.

DAY SEVEN
The Cross

*"They were on the road, going up to Jerusalem, and
Jesus was walking ahead of them; they were amazed,
and those who followed were afraid. He took the twelve
aside again and began to tell them what was to happen
to him, saying, 'See, we are going up to Jerusalem...'"*
—Mark 10: 32-33

Coming Together in the Spirit

On an otherwise normal day, Sister Teresa Benedicta
and her sister Rosa were arrested and deported from the
Carmel in Echt, Holland. It would be some years before
the Carmelite sisters obtained reliable information about
them. On August 9, 1942 she was executed along with
Rosa her sister and so many others at Auschwitz.

Opening Prayer

Are you the sweet song of love
And of holy awe
That eternally resounds around the triune
    throne,
That weds in itself the clear chimes of each
    and every being?

The harmony,
That joins together the members to
    the Head,
In which each one
Finds the mysterious meaning of his
    being blessed
And joyously surges forth,
Freely dissolved in your surging:
Holy Spirit eternal jubilation![1]

RETREAT SESSION SEVEN
Fulfillment in Self-Donation

The burden of the cross that Christ assumed is
corrupted human nature, with the consequences of sin
and suffering to which fallen humanity is subject. The
meaning of the way of the cross is to *carry this burden
out of the world*.[2] Suffering brings us face to face with
ourselves and each other in ways that are impossible to
avoid. Pain gets our attention and forces us to figure
out what we stand for, what God stands for, what life
and death are all about. The answers are not completely
satisfying on an intellectual level. Thus we find ourselves,
reluctantly at first, on a pilgrimage with God through the
worst of what humankind is capable of perpetrating. We
are on a journey with God through the crushing realities
that spring up right in the middle of our lives; sickness,
death and the loss of fortune or friends, opportunities and
dreams. What good meaning could these possibly have?

In the Jewish liturgy for the Feast of Atonement the
reading of the Book of Jonah is important. Jonah, as
you know, was God's reluctant prophet sent to preach

repentance to the Ninevites, a people Jonah deemed
unworthy. Despite God's clear call, the prophet went
in the opposite direction of Nineveh, encountered near
death in a fearsome storm and the belly of a great fish.
Finally, but still without enthusiasm he made his way to
the great city. When the people repented and turned to
God, Jonah was not happy at their salvation, but rather
despaired over the damage his reputation would suffer
when the promised punishment failed to come.

We are all like Jonah to some extent. While God wishes
that all people come to salvation, we would pick and
choose. This is the human corruption to which I referred
before. And it is this limitation of ours that leads to such
suffering among us. What terrible prejudices spring
from our failure to see God's universal love toward all
humankind! Holocausts and genocide are conceived in
the minds and hearts of those who conclude that some
are worthy of respect and some are not. And what of the
terrible pain that comes from this? How can our suffering
have anything to say about hope? When does it become
redemptive?

We must remember that even suffering can be a
manifestation of love. It becomes redemptive when it is
joined mindfully and in complete trust to God's universal
design for all flesh. When all we can do in present
circumstances is accept what suffering brings, we see that
it is a mysterious participation in the accomplishment of
God's purposes. Even when we start out reluctant like
Jonah with half-hearted devotion to God's purposes, our
suffering is nonetheless meaningful.

Much of our suffering is a consequence of human
freedom. In a real sense we are at the mercy of each
other's decision-making capacity. As we know from
history, whole populations can be overcome by the mad
views of their leaders. Those who disagree and work

against evil often do not have the political power to overcome oppression in the short term, or those who can help may not care to make the sacrifice and effort that is necessary. But our response is not passive in this regard. Do you recall the Sermon on the Mount in Matthew's Gospel? Jesus says: "So when you are offering your gift at the altar, if you remember that your brother or sister has something against you, leave your gift there before the altar and go; first be reconciled to your brother or sister, and then come and offer your gift" (Matthew 5: 23-25).

Reconciliation between persons—both individuals and groups—must involve at some point an appropriate remorse and reconciliation on the human plane. The pain that one endures in service to this attempt at understanding and reconciliation demands the best that human efforts can accomplish but ultimately must be put in God's hands. It is at this painful juncture that much suffering may be endured. So far in human history we have not overcome the evil that comes from human freedom. But our sufferings are redemptive when we work to *carry suffering out of this world* through our own loving efforts, prayers and endurance. Do you remember the First Letter of Peter, chapter 3:17-18? Peter writes: "It is better to suffer for doing good, if suffering should be God's will, than to suffer for doing evil. For Christ also suffered for sins once for all, the righteous for the unrighteous, in order to bring you to God." It was to Jerusalem and suffering that Jesus had set his face and found his purpose. His whole life was a pilgrimage. His every thought, word and deed was involved in doing the will of the Father. Like Abraham before him—who was willing to sacrifice his son Isaac; like the Suffering Servant of Isaiah, Jesus too would know rejection, disappointment, failure, torture and death. We who live after the Master know something of the difficult but wondrous result of this total self-donation. We also know that it is a pattern set for all Jesus' followers. Jesus embraced the Cross not to glorify suffering or certainly to condone it, but to show us that total trust, even in the face of suffering, is redemptive. God's purposes are somehow bound up in this most imperfect world still awaiting the fullness of redemption.

I think I knew right from the start of the Third Reich in 1933 what was coming. *During a vacation that year I had returned to the Collegium Marianum after an academic conference. I could not unlock the front door. A kind gentleman noticed my difficulty and after consulting with his wife, invited me to spend the night at their house. These kind people did not know that I was Jewish and were recounting reports from American newspapers regarding cruelties against the Jews in Germany. A light dawned in my brain that once again God had put a heavy hand upon His people and that the fate of this people would also be my own. I thought constantly about the plight of the Jews. I thought that I could travel to Rome to ask the Holy Father Pius XI to issue an encyclical. After inquiries I realized I would have no chance for a private audience. I then presented a request in writing. I know that my letter was delivered unopened to the Holy Father. Some time thereafter I received his blessing for my relatives and me. Nothing else happened. Later on I often wondered whether this letter might have come to his mind once in awhile. For in the years that followed, that which I had predicted came true.*[3]

As I watched some family members flee Germany, and saw the oppression of Jews, my heart was in agony. I could no longer teach, nor was I allowed to speak in public or publish anything. The future was grim. In prayer *I talked with the Savior and told Him that I knew it was His cross that was now being placed upon the Jewish people; that most of them did not understand this, but that those who did, would have to take it up willingly in the name of all. I would do that. He should only show me how.*[4]

My destiny was—in some mysterious way—to
take this suffering out of the world in a humility of
suffering and atonement. The power of God's Presence
and Mercy within the dire circumstances of my life at
that time brought me to this. I went up to Jerusalem, as
it were, with too many others—victims of one of history's
largest campaigns of hatred. I could follow what God was
showing me. Only God can know the deep thoughts, fears,
hopes that lie in the hearts of all. You know, *immediately
before, and for a good while after my conversion, I was of the
opinion that to lead a religious life meant one had to give up all
that was secular and to live totally immersed in thoughts of the
Divine. But gradually I realized that something else is asked
of us in the world and that, even in the contemplative life, one
may not sever the connection with this world. I even believe
that the deeper one is drawn into God, the more one must
"go out of oneself"; that is, one must go to the world in order
to carry the divine life into it.*[5] My service was a simple
and trusting one. In the midst of so much undeserved
suffering I reached out as best I could to those around me
in order to bring some peace and hope. My thoughts and
prayers were always against this horror. How ardently
I wished it had never happened! How deep is my hope
that humankind has learned from it and will assure mass
murder is not repeated!

For Reflection

- *When have you helped others to see the meaning of their suffering?*

- *Is suffering necessary? How much energy do you expend in avoiding it? In accepting it?*

Closing Prayer

To suffer and to be happy although suffering, to have one's feet on the earth, to walk on the dirty and rough paths of this earth and yet to be enthroned with Christ at the Father's right hand, to laugh and cry with the children of this world and ceaselessly sing the praises of God with the choirs of angels—this is the life of the Christian until the morning of eternity breaks forth.[6]

Notes

[1] Edith Stein, *From a Pentecost Novena, The Collected Works of Edith Stein* (Washington, D.C.: ICS Publications, 1989).

[2] Edith Stein, *The Hidden Life: Essays, Meditations, Spiritual Texts,* Volume 4, *The Collected Works of Edith Stein* (Washington, D.C.: ICS Publications, 1992), p. 91.

[3] Susanne M. Batzdorff, *Edith Stein, Selected Writings: With Comments, Reminiscences and Translations of her Poems and Prayers by her Niece* (Springfield, Ill.: Templegate Publishers, 1990), p. 17.

[4] Edith Stein, *Self-Portrait in Letters*, trans., Sr. Josephine Koeppel, O.C.D. (Washington, D.C.: ICS Publications, 1993), p. 353.

[5] Stein, *Self-Portrait in Letters*, p. 54.

[6] Edith Stein, "Love of the Cross," Volume X, *The Collected Works of Edith Stein* (Washington, D.C.: ICS Publications).

Deepening Your Acquaintance

Any good history of the holocaust will help you to ground Edith in the time and circumstances of her life. To continue your acquaintance with Edith specifically, try some of these resources:

Books

Batzdorff, Susanne M. *Aunt Edith: The Jewish Heritage of a Catholic Saint* (Springfield, Ill.: Templegate Publishers, 1998.) Susanne is the niece of Edith Stein.

Herbstrith, Waltraud, ed., and Susanne M. Batzdorff, trans. *Never Forget: Christian and Jewish Perspectives on Edith Stein* (Washington, D.C.: ICS Publications, 1998).

Koeppel, Josephine O.C.D. *Edith Stein: Philosopher and Mystic*, Volume 12, *The Way of the Christian Mystics* (Collegeville, Minn.: Michael Glazier-Liturgical Press, 1990). Sr. Josephine translated *Life in a Jewish Family*, and other works by Edith Stein. She is a Carmelite nun at Elysburg Carmel, Elysburg, Pennsylvania.

Neyer, Maria Amata, O.C.D., *Edith Stein: Her Life in Photos and Documents*, trans. Waltraut Stein, Ph.D. (Washington, D.C.: ICS Publications, 1999.)

Oben, Freda Mary. *Edith Stein, Scholar, Feminist, Saint* (Alba House, N.Y., 1988).

Stein, Edith. *Essays on Woman,* Volume 2, The Collected Works of Edith Stein (Washington, D.C.: ICS Publications, 1987.)

_____. *Life in a Jewish Family: 1891–1916* trans. Josephine Koeppel, O.C.D., Volume 1, The Collected Works of Edith Stein This contains an excellent Chronology and Translator's Afterword.

_____. *Self-Portrait in Letters 1916–1942.* Translated by Josephine Koeppel, O.C.D.,Volume 5 of The Collected Works of Edith Stein (Washington, D.C.: ICS Publications, 1993).